How To Not Blow Up Your Trading Account

A Definitive Guide to Money and Risk Management for Forex Traders

By Erick Vavretchek

"You miss 100% of the shots you don't take"

– Wayne Gretzky

Table of Contents

Acknowledgments

First and foremost I would like to thank my parents and my twin sister for all the support I had through my whole life. No matter what I chose to do. All I always heard was: "Go for it, you can do whatever you want. We will always be here!" Nothing can go much wrong when you have that kind of love. Speaking of love I would also want to thank my wife for the support and understanding of the thousands of hours spent in development and understanding of the markets and especially for the many times she asked me: "Oh wow, where are you copying that from?" lol. Funny, but true.

I could not forget my trading friends, Alan D, Angela A, Angela D, Brent, CK, Colleen, Dan, Lynne, Paul C, Phil, Steve H and many others. This is a journey better not taken alone. We grow together.

To all the charlatans in this market that have some of my money, I owe you a big thank you too. I fell for your tricks too many times, I was naïve and it was a hard path to go through without guidance or with the wrong one. I learnt so much from you and your dishonesty. It definitely made me a better man and trader. I am sure you will meet Karma one day.

Foreword

As you're here reading this book you probably already realise that there's no holy grail trading strategy; that ALL technical analysis works in isolation now and then - but that to be a consistently profitable trader you have to combine disciplined technical analysis with sound trader psychology and proper money management.

You'll discover in this book that there is both a science and an art to money management. What works best for you boils down to your personality, your cash flow preferences and risk profile as a trader.

Personally, I prefer to keep most of my available trading funds in a government regulated savings account with only a small amount in my trading account, leveraged at 1:400, which is on the high side. I also pay myself at the end of each week when my account is in profit. I do this for three main reasons:

1. I prefer the safety of a bank account for the majority of my funds and the high-leverage of the broker account I've chosen which gives me

access to ample funds should I need them. My bank account is sufficient to cover any properly managed drawdown so I'm not margin-called. This setup gives me security and flexibility.

2. My risk profile and trader psychology responds best to cash flow. Treating my trading as a business that rewards me with an income (rather than compounding my account), motivates me.

3. Siphoning my profits off to my bank account saves me from "testosterone trading" when I'm on a winning streak and prone to over-confidence with my position sizes!

Whether you prefer to pay yourself, compound your profits, use larger leverage, smaller leverage or multiple accounts over different brokers, "How To Not Blow Up Your Trading Account" will give you the fundamentals for a money management strategy that could keep you in the game long enough to find your trading "edge" and profit handsomely from it.

By **Danielle Lehrer**
Trader & Co-founder of ForexNation.org
The World's 1st Not-For-Profit Broker

Intro

We cannot start talking about trading before we lay down the money and risk management cards. We always hear about buy low and sell high when people talk about trading in general. The fact is that many trades will go even lower after your buy order. When enough is enough? When should you take the loss and move on? How big will you lose? These are few of the many questions I will try to answer in this book.

How much are you willing to risk per trade? How much money can you hand to the markets and not lose your sleep, your house and your wife? This is a pretty serious game. Whenever money is involved you will find professionals. These professionals are waiting to take your money, they often are a lot more patient than you. Although sometimes very well regulated, there is no ethic whatsoever in this business. Every participant is in it to make money. It is a zero sum game, meaning that there is a loser for every winner. Think about that.

Another pretty harsh statistic tells that only 5% of traders are profitable. I know what you are thinking. The exact thought in your mind right now is: "I will dedicate myself and I know I will be in the 5% group, I am a successful professional with many awards". One of the good things about trading is that the market does not interview you, you will not have to show your diploma or bring your CV, the market could not care less about who you are and what you know. Nothing is personal. The plumber, the footballer, the beautician, the lawyer, the engineer, the builder and the doctor are all levelled off in the trading arena and their chances are the same. So sorry to tell you, but you might not succeed in this business. And if you do it will take some time. Do not give up!

So what the 95% crowd does not know that the fortunate rest have mastered? This is not a simple question, but there are 3 subjects when it comes to trading and all of them must be totally understood by you if you want to have a crack of moving to the smaller group of successful traders. The 3 key components are trading system, psychology and money management and I will be addressing the last one. Fully understand it and you will keep your shirt on, your sleep, house and wife.

What Is Money Management & Risk Management

It is normal to read about Risk and Money Management as if they were the same thing. Although I like to think of Risk Management as being part of Money Management, which in its way is a much broader topic.

Risk Management can easily be described as the process of analysing a trade before the execution: Can you tick all the checklist boxes regarding the setup? How far is your Stop Loss? Is it too big for your capital and risk tolerance? How do you grade the trade? Does it give you a healthy risk to reward ratio? How many trades do I have already open, can I afford to add risk to the portfolio?

Those are the types of questions you may ask yourself before pulling the trigger on a trade. Those questions will determine whether the risk involved aligns with your trading plan.

But it does not stop there. After a trade is placed you must constantly monitor its risk: Are there any important news releases that may affect the trade already in place? Is the trade playing up nicely and already in profit, isn't it time to move your Stop Loss to another safe place and reduce the risk on the trade? The trade is already at a break even point where no matter what happens you cannot lose money on it any longer. You have zero risk involved, so you may consider adding to the position. In this way you can maximise your gains having your risk always under control.

You can also rate your trades' setup as perfect and nearly perfect (you will not trade if the setup is not a least a nearly perfect one, will you?). You can then use a full position size for the perfect setup (2% for instance) and half position size (1%) for the nearly perfect setup, in this way you risk more in the trade you believe has more chances to work out as planned.

It is fair to say that in Risk Management your only concern is the risk you are exposed to and it is part of Money Management.

Money Management is how you manage your money as a whole and not only how you watch your risk. It includes investment, banking, taxes and budgeting and it is also known as investment management.

Investment covers your trading plan, having the risk management within it. But you also must be aware that you will need to pay taxes on capital gains. You must have this money available for the tax man every year or you may find yourself in big trouble.

You will find more about Banking and Budgeting in the "Trading Account vs. Bank Account" chapter.

Why Is It So Important

Let me start with that: no matter how good of a trader you are, you will not progress unless you have mastered your Risk and Money Management. I dare to say that you cannot even be considered a good trader if you have not accomplished the above stated.

How much can your risk? How will you risk it? Where is your money? The answers of these questions are on the tip of the tongue for any professional trader.

A good Risk Management in place can turn a good trading system into an excellent system. Maybe even more important, it can make you survive a long enough period with a bad system, long enough to make you realise the system is not tradable. You will have time to pull the plug and start over with enough money to trade a different system.

There are only so many mistakes you can make in the Forex Business and believe me, you will make mistakes. Entering a trade in the wrong pair, press the Sell button when you actually wanted to Buy, place your stop in the wrong place because you mistyped the price or forget to add a Stop Loss order at all. I am sure with time you will come up with a lot more.

Having a solid Risk Management in place and executing it flawlessly is paramount to survive in the markets. This is the variant that you can control, amongst many other that you simply cannot. So make sure you master the subject and you will be in the right path to trading successfully.

Why Traders Lose Money

Traders lose money because they treat their trading like a hobby. It can be fun and addictive to stare at pretty charts and place random bets. That is why poking machines are so popular and people continue to over and over lose their salary / pension in this money making machines.

Gambling and trading are very similar activities, but there is a subtle, although crucial difference between them. When you gamble you know how much money you are risking. Do not get me wrong here, this will not stop the gambler to lose all his money. But when you are in the Casino, if the roulette does not stop where you placed your chips, those chips are gone. No more than the ones you placed.

Whereas if you do not have a money management in place, one trade only can do a lot of damage. When a trade goes against you, you are responsible for taking the loss. No one will do it for you. So you'd better have your stops in place and never move them against you.

There is in fact another difference between gambling and trading. In the casino the rules are dictated by the house and when you are trading the markets the house is you. You decide when to enter the markets and when to get out. You set the probabilities, you make them work in your favour. You know the chances of a given pattern that you have studied to succeed, you know how much you risk on that given trade. You have control of your movements.

Get your money management right and remember that practice makes perfect. Take your time to develop your trading psychology it is extremely important. If 10 different traders are told to open a position with a given Stop Loss and Take Profit, none of them are likely to have the same results. Some will get scared when the trade moves against them and close the position, some will wait until it gets to their entry price to close at break even. Everyone will have a reason to manage the trade differently. And those without the discipline, the proper money management and good trading psychology skills will most likely lose money, even if the trade turns out to reach the Take Profit Level.

As I mentioned in the introductory chapter, the 3 essential skills to be developed are: Trading System, Money Management and Trading Psychology. Think of it as a three legged stool. If one is missing you are prone to fail.

Always remember that trading is a business and should be treated like one. Have your blue print, called trading plan. Make sure you are capitalised and can survive the start up period where you are likely to incur some losses. Take care of the losses with a good Money Management. Take a deep breath and believe in yourself.

Leverage And Margin, Finally Understand What It Is And How It Affects Your Trading

Understanding margin is essential if you want to trade Forex and manage your money properly. You need to be aware of the benefits that leverage can bring to you, but especially be aware of the dangers that trading with margin represents. You will soon understand while margins is said to be a double-edged sword.

There are many types of leverage available to you, being able to choose the right one and understand what it means is paramount to your success, being when you are starting and need to make sure you will not get a margin call in your first trade or when you become a professional trader and utilises the power of leverage to manage your money more efficiently.

Unless you live in the USA, where maximum margin available for US Citizens is 50:1, you can choose from 1:1 to 500:1.

To make it an easy to understand example, we are assuming our account is held in USD and we are trading a pair where USD is the Quote currency.

But what does it mean? It means that if you have a 100:1 margin, for every $1 dollar in your account you can control $100 dollars. You leverage your money, you are able to control much more money than what you actually have.

When you trade with margin you are taking a loan from your Broker, on which interest rates will incur, positive or negative (depending whether your are long or short and what pair you are trading) when you hold positions overnight. In Forex this is known as Swap.

Margin works as a security deposit on your loan that is returned to you after you close your trade (in common terms, when you pay back the loan). Let's imagine you open a $1000 account with leverage 100:1. You then decide to buy 0.5 lot of EURUSD (or 5 minis), it represents 50,000 of the quote currency. You should now be asking, how can I buy 50,000 USD if I only have 1,000 in my account. The reason you were able to execute this trade was the leverage you have in your account. By having a 100:1 leverage when you bought 0.5 lot of EURUSD, which is 50,000, a deposit was held as margin, the margin being used in order to let you trade the 0.5 lot is: 50,000 / 100(your leverage) = 500.

So our $1000 account now has $500 being used as margin, which leaves us with another $500 available to trade (to be used as margin), also referred as free margin. Your free margin is your equity (Total balance + Open positions) – margin used.

Sweet! You may think: I still have $500 available to trade and have a $50,000 position, I will open another $50,000 by buying 0.5 lot of GBPUSD now. You then proceed with your (not so) brilliant idea. What happens next is what have already happened to many of us (me included). After your second position is open your free margin drops instantly to 0,00 (assuming your positions are still not losing or making any money), remember the formula:

Free margin = Equity – Margin Used → $1000 – ($500 - $500) = 0.

You probably have an idea of what is coming next, you from now on cannot open any other position until you close some of the open ones to free some margin for you. It is a pretty bad situation to find your self into. But things are about to become a bit worse. You had no idea there was a major news announcement schedule for the next 30 minutes. Today is

Non-Farm Payroll Friday and markets will go crazy after the numbers announcement. Things are not looking good for you, the numbers revealed show a bad situation for the US economy, you for a split of a second see you 2 currency pairs being traded gain few pips, but unexpectedly a strong sell off takes control of the market and you are now in negative territory. Your free margin is now less than 0, because your equity is less than $1000 now and you still have $1000 being held as margin. Your platform starts blinking red. Your broker is not happy with your current positions and is giving you a warning your free margin is now negative, remember you are leveraged and if the markets continue to plunge you are at risk of losing more than what you have.

It varies from broker to broker, but you will normally receive a warning when you free margin is below 0 and you will get a margin call once your Account equity = Required Margin x 30%. E.g. $1000 x 30% = $300. When your Equity drops to $300 dollars you will have all your positions closed immediately. You will have no chance. The broker will close the positions for a total loss of $700 dollars. If this was your first day trading. Welcome to the club. Situation is normally a bit worse in real life situation where Slippage, Commissions and Swap rates will also consume some of your capital.

It is really important for you to understand the maths from the example above as it will vary depending on many factors, leverage being the most important. If you for instance have a 400:1 leverage in the same scenario you would only be using $250 margin to keep the positions. So a margin call at 30% would leave you with $75 dollars left in your account, much bigger loss, but in the other hand market would need to move even further against your before the margin call was triggered. If you had a 50:1, which most of American citizens have, in this case you would not be allowed to open the second position as the first one would take $1000 in margin alone.

It is all a matter of common sense and understanding, you can come up with a unlimited number of scenarios and as long as your understand what is going on you will not be caught by surprise.

Please take your time to read this chapter again, but now with pen and paper and try to understand and create some hypothetical scenarios. It is very simple once you try and understand it. Believe me it will be worth your while.

Read more on the next chapter how you can smartly use margin in your favour by applying good money management.

Trading Account Vs. Bank Account

You are probably wondering what your Trading Account has to do with your Bank Account. I tell you: a whole lot!

This book is mostly focused on not losing money. I know many traders that can get great return rates on their accounts to then give everything back later. So no matter how much money you can make if you do not know how to keep it.

To protect your capital is your utmost objective in this business and following that is to make it grow. Never forget! Always think about how much money you can lose in a trade BEFORE you start to contemplate the possible gains. If the risk is too big, simply pass it, there will always be another trade.

Now that you understand enough about margin you know that you can trade big amounts of cash without actually having it. With a 400:1 leverage account you only need

$250 to control a $100,000 position, or in simpler terms, one full lot.

Great! If you are about to start in the Forex business or you are an experienced trader. You have some cash available to trade with, some cash that your life or your rent / mortgage do not depend on. For illustration purpose let's make up a number for the account: $10,000.00.

This is a valid argument for anyone that cares about their money, newbie or veteran, so bare with me and you will soon understand where we are getting into.

You call your Forex Broker to get you new account started and transfer your $10,000 to it. So you are set, waiting for your next trade.

A long opportunity appears and, with everything you learnt here you decide to risk 1% of your account in the trade. You define that a safe position for your Stop Loss is 35 pips, few pips below your last swing low with great past support. To make our lives easier here, let's assume your account is in USD, the trade that you are just about to open is in the EURUSD and we are not worried about commission, swap or slippage (I still dream about the ideal scenario):

Risk: $10,000 * 1% = $100
Stop Loss: 35 pips
Value per pip: $100 / 35 pips = $2.8571428 per pip
Position size: $2.85 / 10 = 0.28 lots

So know you open the position, long EURUSD with a position size of 0.28 (notice that all the rounding in the maths operations above were rounded to the immediate lower number). You know can rest assured that if you get stopped out you will lose $98, very close, but under the $100 or 1% you were willing to risk in the trade.

What you must also notice is the margin that was held from your account in order to keep that trade open. If you have:

400:1 Leverage Account: Margin used → $70
100:1 Leverage Account: Margin used → $280
50:1 Leverage Account: Margin used → $560

If you are following me, from your $10,000 account with your broker you are using, in the worst scenario, if you are a USA resident abiding to the CFTC (Commodity Futures Trading Commission) rule of 50:1, $560 for margin and are risking $100, bringing your total money in use to $660.

That leaves your account with an idle balance of $9,340 ($10,000 - $660). I do not know about you, but I think it is a lot of money to leave with your Broker when it is definitely not needed to trade. Even if you have 5 positions open at the same time with similar characteristics that will bring your idle money to $6700 and your risk to 5% (5 positions with 1% Risk each).

You probably know by now where we are heading to. Very recently (I am writing this book in 2013) we had major Brokers going bankrupt and taking clients' money with them. Money that should be held in segregated accounts, money that should never have been used by the Brokers. These recent Scandals involved MF Global and PFG Best and thousand of traders were left with nothing, fighting to recoup some or all of their money.

Mind you that these Brokers were fully regulated and ran by known personalities in the financial arena. This did not make any difference. So the best place to keep your money is in your bank and not at your Brokers. I, myself, never had any problems with Brokers (knock on wood), but I would be foolish to not worry about it.

Depending on your account size, your leverage and your trading plan (how many trades are you allowed to have at anytime), you should only leave with your broker enough money to cover the costs and the rest of it in a savings bank account, preferably one that pays interest rates on your deposit. You gain nothing with the money parked with your Broker plus you may be victim of a bad broker. My rule of thumb is, if you have:

400:1 Leverage Account: 15% with broker 85% in a savings account.
100:1 Leverage Account: 30% with broker 70% in a savings account.
50:1 Leverage Account: 50% with broker 50% in a savings account.

To wrap up this chapter, $10,000 is your trading capital. Trading capital being the money you have available for trading. It consists in Savings Account balance + Broker account balance. If your trading capital is $10,000 and your margin is 400:1, this means you will have $1,500 (15%) in your trading account and $8,500 (85%) at your bank in a savings account receiving interest payments.

These numbers must always be in check, if you have been through a tough period and have incurred some losses you must need to transfer some of your money from the savings account to your broker account. Totalise your trading capital and redistribute it after few a period. Make sure if you have enough money to trade your plan with your Broker and no more than that. Gain bank interest rates in your deposit account and play safe.

In the Essential Tool for Trading chapter you will be introduced to a tool that is capable of calculating your position size automatically, taking into account your Trading Capital (Bank Deposit + Broker Balance). It is not free, but it has a very affordable price and you will not be able to live without it.

Position Size

Different traders have different risk tolerance and this is due to experience, account size and psychology level. If you are starting now I recommend 0.5%. This means that you are only risking 0.5% of your balance in every trade. For instance, if you have a $1000 account and you lose a trade you will only lose $5. This will ensure that your account will live through tough periods when you are learning or when you are off to a losing streak, it will happen.

With a 0.5% risk you will have to lose 200 trades in a row to lose your whole account. In fact it is a bit better than that, given that if you always follow you 0.5% risk, your losing trades will become smaller at the same proportion that your account shrinks.

To be precise, after 200 losing trades in a row, your account will be reduced from $1000 to $366.96 (Table 1).

Table 1 – 200 losses in a row with 0.5% risk

Trades	Balance	0.5% Loss	Trades	Balance	0.5% Loss
1	1000.000	5.000	27	877.809	4.389
2	995.000	4.975	28	873.420	4.367
3	990.025	4.950	29	869.053	4.345
4	985.075	4.925	30	864.708	4.324
5	980.150	4.901	31	860.384	4.302
6	975.249	4.876	32	856.082	4.280
7	970.373	4.852	33	851.802	4.259
8	965.521	4.828	34	847.543	4.238
9	960.693	4.803	35	843.305	4.217
10	955.890	4.779	36	839.089	4.195
11	951.110	4.756	37	834.893	4.174
12	946.355	4.732	38	830.719	4.154
13	941.623	4.708	39	826.565	4.133
14	936.915	4.685	40	822.432	4.112
15	932.230	4.661	41	818.320	4.092
16	927.569	4.638	42	814.229	4.071
17	922.931	4.615	43	810.157	4.051
18	918.316	4.592	44	806.107	4.031
19	913.725	4.569	45	802.076	4.010
20	909.156	4.546	46	798.066	3.990
21	904.610	4.523	47	794.075	3.970
22	900.087	4.500	48	790.105	3.951
23	895.587	4.478	49	786.154	3.931
24	891.109	4.456	50	782.224	3.911
25	886.654	4.433	51	778.313	3.892
26	882.220	4.411	52	774.421	3.872

Trades	Balance	0.5% Loss	Trades	Balance	0.5% Loss
53	770.549	3.853	80	673.013	3.365
54	766.696	3.833	81	669.648	3.348
55	762.863	3.814	82	666.300	3.331
56	759.048	3.795	83	662.968	3.315
57	755.253	3.776	84	659.653	3.298
58	751.477	3.757	85	656.355	3.282
59	747.719	3.739	86	653.073	3.265
60	743.981	3.720	87	649.808	3.249
61	740.261	3.701	88	646.559	3.233
62	736.560	3.683	89	643.326	3.217
63	732.877	3.664	90	640.109	3.201
64	729.212	3.646	91	636.909	3.185
65	725.566	3.628	92	633.724	3.169
66	721.939	3.610	93	630.556	3.153
67	718.329	3.592	94	627.403	3.137
68	714.737	3.574	95	624.266	3.121
69	711.164	3.556	96	621.145	3.106
70	707.608	3.538	97	618.039	3.090
71	704.070	3.520	98	614.949	3.075
72	700.549	3.503	99	611.874	3.059
73	697.047	3.485	100	608.815	3.044
74	693.561	3.468	101	605.770	3.029
75	690.094	3.450	102	602.742	3.014
76	686.643	3.433	103	599.728	2.999
77	683.210	3.416	104	596.729	2.984
78	679.794	3.399	105	593.746	2.969
79	676.395	3.382	106	590.777	2.954

Trades	Balance	0.5% Loss	Trades	Balance	0.5% Loss
107	587.823	2.939	134	513.416	2.567
108	584.884	2.924	135	510.849	2.554
109	581.959	2.910	136	508.295	2.541
110	579.050	2.895	137	505.754	2.529
111	576.154	2.881	138	503.225	2.516
112	573.274	2.866	139	500.709	2.504
113	570.407	2.852	140	498.205	2.491
114	567.555	2.838	141	495.714	2.479
115	564.717	2.824	142	493.236	2.466
116	561.894	2.809	143	490.769	2.454
117	559.084	2.795	144	488.316	2.442
118	556.289	2.781	145	485.874	2.429
119	553.508	2.768	146	483.445	2.417
120	550.740	2.754	147	481.027	2.405
121	547.986	2.740	148	478.622	2.393
122	545.246	2.726	149	476.229	2.381
123	542.520	2.713	150	473.848	2.369
124	539.808	2.699	151	471.479	2.357
125	537.108	2.686	152	469.121	2.346
126	534.423	2.672	153	466.776	2.334
127	531.751	2.659	154	464.442	2.322
128	529.092	2.645	155	462.120	2.311
129	526.447	2.632	156	459.809	2.299
130	523.814	2.619	157	457.510	2.288
131	521.195	2.606	158	455.222	2.276
132	518.589	2.593	159	452.946	2.265
133	515.996	2.580	160	450.682	2.253

Trades	Balance	0.5% Loss	Trades	Balance	0.5% Loss
161	448.428	2.242	181	405.653	2.028
162	446.186	2.231	182	403.625	2.018
163	443.955	2.220	183	401.606	2.008
164	441.735	2.209	184	399.598	1.998
165	439.527	2.198	185	397.600	1.988
166	437.329	2.187	186	395.612	1.978
167	435.142	2.176	187	393.634	1.968
168	432.967	2.165	188	391.666	1.958
169	430.802	2.154	189	389.708	1.949
170	428.648	2.143	190	387.759	1.939
171	426.505	2.133	191	385.821	1.929
172	424.372	2.122	192	383.891	1.919
173	422.250	2.111	193	381.972	1.910
174	420.139	2.101	194	380.062	1.900
175	418.038	2.090	195	378.162	1.891
176	415.948	2.080	196	376.271	1.881
177	413.868	2.069	197	374.390	1.872
178	411.799	2.059	198	372.518	1.863
179	409.740	2.049	199	370.655	1.853
180	407.691	2.038	200	368.802	1.844

This is due to compounding, it is worth to mention that it also works in your favour. Let's say that instead of losing 200 trades in a row you win 200 trades in a row, in this case your account will grow from $1000 to $2711.52, a whopping 172% increase (Table 2).

Table 2 – 200 wins in a row with 0.5% risk

Trades	Balance	0.5% Win	Trades	Balance	0.5% Win
1	1000.000	5.000	21	1104.896	5.524
2	1005.000	5.025	22	1110.420	5.552
3	1010.025	5.050	23	1115.972	5.580
4	1015.075	5.075	24	1121.552	5.608
5	1020.151	5.101	25	1127.160	5.636
6	1025.251	5.126	26	1132.796	5.664
7	1030.378	5.152	27	1138.460	5.692
8	1035.529	5.178	28	1144.152	5.721
9	1040.707	5.204	29	1149.873	5.749
10	1045.911	5.230	30	1155.622	5.778
11	1051.140	5.256	31	1161.400	5.807
12	1056.396	5.282	32	1167.207	5.836
13	1061.678	5.308	33	1173.043	5.865
14	1066.986	5.335	34	1178.908	5.895
15	1072.321	5.362	35	1184.803	5.924
16	1077.683	5.388	36	1190.727	5.954
17	1083.071	5.415	37	1196.681	5.983
18	1088.487	5.442	38	1202.664	6.013
19	1093.929	5.470	39	1208.677	6.043
20	1099.399	5.497	40	1214.721	6.074

Trades	Balance	0.5% Win	Trades	Balance	0.5% Win
41	1220.794	6.104	69	1403.758	7.019
42	1226.898	6.134	70	1410.777	7.054
43	1233.033	6.165	71	1417.831	7.089
44	1239.198	6.196	72	1424.920	7.125
45	1245.394	6.227	73	1432.044	7.160
46	1251.621	6.258	74	1439.204	7.196
47	1257.879	6.289	75	1446.401	7.232
48	1264.168	6.321	76	1453.633	7.268
49	1270.489	6.352	77	1460.901	7.305
50	1276.842	6.384	78	1468.205	7.341
51	1283.226	6.416	79	1475.546	7.378
52	1289.642	6.448	80	1482.924	7.415
53	1296.090	6.480	81	1490.339	7.452
54	1302.571	6.513	82	1497.790	7.489
55	1309.083	6.545	83	1505.279	7.526
56	1315.629	6.578	84	1512.806	7.564
57	1322.207	6.611	85	1520.370	7.602
58	1328.818	6.644	86	1527.971	7.640
59	1335.462	6.677	87	1535.611	7.678
60	1342.139	6.711	88	1543.289	7.716
61	1348.850	6.744	89	1551.006	7.755
62	1355.594	6.778	90	1558.761	7.794
63	1362.372	6.812	91	1566.555	7.833
64	1369.184	6.846	92	1574.387	7.872
65	1376.030	6.880	93	1582.259	7.911
66	1382.910	6.915	94	1590.171	7.951
67	1389.825	6.949	95	1598.122	7.991
68	1396.774	6.984	96	1606.112	8.031

Trades	Balance	0.5% Win	Trades	Balance	0.5% Win
97	1614.143	8.071	125	1856.058	9.280
98	1622.213	8.111	126	1865.339	9.327
99	1630.324	8.152	127	1874.665	9.373
100	1638.476	8.192	128	1884.039	9.420
101	1646.668	8.233	129	1893.459	9.467
102	1654.902	8.275	130	1902.926	9.515
103	1663.176	8.316	131	1912.441	9.562
104	1671.492	8.357	132	1922.003	9.610
105	1679.850	8.399	133	1931.613	9.658
106	1688.249	8.441	134	1941.271	9.706
107	1696.690	8.483	135	1950.978	9.755
108	1705.174	8.526	136	1960.732	9.804
109	1713.699	8.568	137	1970.536	9.853
110	1722.268	8.611	138	1980.389	9.902
111	1730.879	8.654	139	1990.291	9.951
112	1739.534	8.698	140	2000.242	10.001
113	1748.231	8.741	141	2010.243	10.051
114	1756.973	8.785	142	2020.295	10.101
115	1765.757	8.829	143	2030.396	10.152
116	1774.586	8.873	144	2040.548	10.203
117	1783.459	8.917	145	2050.751	10.254
118	1792.376	8.962	146	2061.005	10.305
119	1801.338	9.007	147	2071.310	10.357
120	1810.345	9.052	148	2081.666	10.408
121	1819.397	9.097	149	2092.074	10.460
122	1828.494	9.142	150	2102.535	10.513
123	1837.636	9.188	151	2113.048	10.565
124	1846.824	9.234	152	2123.613	10.618

Trades	Balance	0.5% Win	Trades	Balance	0.5% Win
153	2134.231	10.671	177	2405.619	12.028
154	2144.902	10.725	178	2417.647	12.088
155	2155.626	10.778	179	2429.735	12.149
156	2166.405	10.832	180	2441.884	12.209
157	2177.237	10.886	181	2454.094	12.270
158	2188.123	10.941	182	2466.364	12.332
159	2199.063	10.995	183	2478.696	12.393
160	2210.059	11.050	184	2491.089	12.455
161	2221.109	11.106	185	2503.545	12.518
162	2232.215	11.161	186	2516.062	12.580
163	2243.376	11.217	187	2528.643	12.643
164	2254.593	11.273	188	2541.286	12.706
165	2265.866	11.329	189	2553.992	12.770
166	2277.195	11.386	190	2566.762	12.834
167	2288.581	11.443	191	2579.596	12.898
168	2300.024	11.500	192	2592.494	12.962
169	2311.524	11.558	193	2605.457	13.027
170	2323.081	11.615	194	2618.484	13.092
171	2334.697	11.673	195	2631.576	13.158
172	2346.370	11.732	196	2644.734	13.224
173	2358.102	11.791	197	2657.958	13.290
174	2369.893	11.849	198	2671.248	13.356
175	2381.742	11.909	199	2684.604	13.423
176	2393.651	11.968	200	2698.027	13.490

Not Bad! Even Albert Einstein was fascinated about the power of compounding interest, so much so, that he came up with something that he called the magic number. This number is 72. If you divide 72 by the fixed interest rate for a given period you will get the number of period it will take to double the initial sum.

Interesting, isn't it? Let's say your bank gives you 6% interest per year in your investment. You divide 72 by 6. It will give you 12. Twelve is the number of years that it will take for your account to double if you keep it in the bank at the given interest rate (Table 3).

Table 3 - Albert Einstein Magic Number Example: at the end of the 12th year your balance would be 2012.20, just over 100%.

Years	Balance	Interest Paid (6% per year)
1	1000.00	60.00
2	1060.00	63.60
3	1123.60	67.42
4	1191.02	71.46
5	1262.48	75.75
6	1338.23	80.29
7	1418.52	85.11
8	1503.63	90.22
9	1593.85	95.63
10	1689.48	101.37
11	1790.85	107.45
12	1898.30	113.90

I hope you understood why Einstein was so fascinated about compounding interest. Mind you that we used 0.5% in our example. Some experienced traders risk up to %5 per trade. The exponential growth you would obtain from it would be astonishing. I know that in no time you will be an expert in compounding calculations and will be telling everyone how quickly you can turn $1,000.00 into $1,000,000.00.

Let me tell you something, yes it is possible, but you will not risk enough to make it, at least not in your first years in the business. I live by the risk small, slow and stead growth theory. So if you are paying attention to what I am saying you will not risk 5% per trade and another good advice is to not tell anyone that you are in this business, if you can resist. This will bring extra pressure that you do not need. Multiplying money is a very exciting thing and your friends will be very interested in what you are doing, although they will say that you are crazy for putting you money there, they will ask you on a daily basis: "Did you make money today?". So master what you are doing before telling people what you can do. Not to mention the number of people wanting to give you money to trade for them, do not fall for the trap. Not until you have at least 2 years track record to prove that you are doing the right thing. Believe me, if you have 2 years records to back you up, you will get more money to trade that you can think about. Trading for others is difficult.

Enough of advice, this should be about position size, but I got carried away with compound interest and what you should not do.

Position size is you how much you buy or sell when you place a trade. Everyone is used to stocks, so I believe an analogy can help here. Stocks are based in Unit, so you buy 3 units IBM stocks and sell 1 unit of Apple stock. Those are your position size. You know the price of the stock so it is just a matter of multiplying the value by the number of bought or sold units to find out how much money is in play. But in the Forex business we are buying and selling money, so the question is how much money. The amounts of money we trade are quantised in lots.

What is a lot? 1 lot is equivalent of $100,000 dollars of the given currency, so when you buy 1 Lot you are buying $100,000.00 of the currency you are trading. It is a big number, but thanks to leverage and margin you can buy the whole lot with considerable small amount in your account (Check the Margin Chapter to understand leverage better).

I am assuming that everyone here knows what a Pip is, and how currency pairs are quoted, but it is OK if you do not know. It is quite an easy explanation and I will address this in an extra chapter at the end of the book, so I make sure I got you covered. If you do not know what a Pip is, take a quick look at the last chapter and come back here as soon as you finish.

In order to begin with an easy explanation, let's consider that you have an account in USD, and your balance, for explanation purposes, is irrelevant. You see a good opportunity to open a trade and enter the market, you then buy 1 lot of EURUSD. This means, as you must know, that you are betting on the rise of the EURO and devaluation of the USD, hence you want the quoted price to go up. Your position size being 1 lot means that you have 100,000.00 USD in play. Your position size can also be said to be 100,000 or simply 100k. The EURUSD price when you opened your buy trade was 1.3000 and the price quickly rose to 1.3015. What you have now is a 15 pips profit sitting on the table and if you close your position now this is your profit:

Bought Position (open):
$100.000 x 1.3000 = $130,000
Sold Position (close):
$100.000 x 1.3015 = $130,150
Profit:
$130,150 − $130.000 = $150
You have just made $150. If you divide this by the profit in pips you get:
$150 / 15 pips = $10 per pip

This is the value per pip when your position size is 1 lot and the quote currency of the pair you are trading is the same currency as your trading account.

In the next chapter we will analyse position size calculation in greater detail.

Details On How To Calculate Position Size And Value Per Pip Based On Your Risk

In the previous chapter I showed you an easy way to calculate your position size assuming that the currency you hold your account at and the quote of the pair you are trading are the same. For instance, trading account in USD and pair being traded being EURUSD. It is a lot easier when we have an ideal situation.

Just to recap that, let's say your account balance is 1000 USD and you see an opportunity to trade GBPUSD with the stop loss order 30 pips away from your entry. At this time it looks like a perfect setup and you want to risk 2% of your account in this particular trade, the formula we are going to use is:

> **Position Size = (Risk / Stop Loss in Pips) / 10**
> 2% of 1000USD = 1000 x 0.02 = 20 → your risk is 20USD
> 20 USD / 30 pips = 20 / 30 = 0.66 → Value per pip must be 0.66USD
> 0.66 / 10 = 0.066 → Position size will be 0.066, but it must have 2 decimal digits only, so you will round it to the next lower number → 0.06 (Or 6 micros or 6k)

By applying this simple formula we found our position size, rounded it to the next lower number 0.06, in this ideal scenario we have $0.60 per pip. So if your Stop Loss gets hit and you get taken out of the trade at a loss you will lose:

> 0.60USD x 30pips(Stop Loss) = 18USD → Just under the 2% risk we decided we would accept, PERFECT!

That was a nice and simple exercise, the only problem is that things are far from ideal in the real world. Depending on where you live you will have you account held in a different currency so you would not be subjected to major fluctuations. Not only that, but you will not limit yourself to trade only currency pairs where the quote currency is the same as you account. You will, most likely, trade any currency pair that is moving nicely and presenting you a perfect or near perfect setup. That implies that the formula we used later no longer applies to you.

For the next exercise we will assume that you have an account of 10,000AUD and found a perfect trade setup on the EURJPY. Now we have our account in AUD and the quote currency is JPY. After further analysis you decided that your Stop Loss will be 70 pips away from your entry, giving your trade some space to evolve. You decided to risk 2% on this trade so your risk is 200AUD.

The first thing to do find the conversion rate from you account balance currency (AUD) to the quote currency (JPY). We can simply check the on our trading platform for AUDJPY to get the conversion rate, right now in my charts I can see it is 83.20.

The formula will be:

Position Size = (Risk in Quote Currency / Stop Loss in Pips) / Divider

Where Divider depends on the quote pair:
For quote pair JPY, our divider is 1000 for other currency pairs divider is 10.
200 AUD(your risk) * 83.20 (conversion rate) = 16,640→ your risk is 16,640 JPY
16,640 JPY / 70 pips = 16,640 / 70 = 237.714 →
Value per pip must be 237.714 JPY
237.714 JPY / 1000 = 0.2377 → Position Size will be 0.23 (also know as 23 micro lots, 2.3 mini lot or 23K)

In the example above, if your Stop Loss gets hit, you will lose just under 2% of your balance, as it should be. If you reverse the calculation above you will find out the loss was actually 193.51 AUD, achieving this by using our conservative approach of rounding the position size to the next lower value.

Some times you will not find the exact pair in your platform to get the conversion rate. To illustrate this scenario consider your account is in AUD and you are trading USDSEK. You check your platform but there is no AUDSEK or SEKAUD for you the get the conversion rate, what you then need to do, is to first convert your risk to USD by looking at AUDUSD and then to SEK with USDSEK itself. From that on you will have your risk in the quote currency (SEK) and can proceed normally to the formula previously explained. It just add another math to the process.

This is the most important thing that this book is teaching you, no matter how far is your Stop Loss, 30 pips, 70 pips or 250pips, once you have decided your risk per trade (based on your trading plan, quality of the setup and trading strategy) and apply the formula to find the correct Position Size, you can rest assured that you will be taken out of the trade and will lose only what your were initially willing to risk.

If you ventured through this chapter and understood everything I had to explain to you, well done, you deserve a treat as a reward for your dedication and focus. Whenever we have Account Currency equals Quote of traded pair we know that 1 lot equals to $10/pip and 0.1 lot equals $1/pip. It could not be simpler than that. The complicated stuff is when the quote is different, I develop a hack that make the calculation a lot simpler. Let's use the USDSEK for this example. Right now it is trading at 6.6958. The hack is very simple we need to mathematically inverse this number to get a number we can work with:

> The inverse of x is 1 / x. So the inverse of 6.6958 is 1 / 6.6958 = 0.1493.

You just found the value per pip in USD for 0.1 lot traded of USDSEK, about 15 cents. Or 0.149 USD. Now if your account is in JPY you simply convert this using the USDJPY now priced at 79.889. So the value per pip in JPY for 0.1 lot of USDSEK traded is 0.1493 * 79.889 = 11.93 yens.

This is the simplest way to calculate value per pip and most likely the first time you stumble upon this calculation too. This is my cheat version of the complicated stuff we had to go through in order to fully understand the maths behind it. Take this little hack with you and be diligent about your position size and never lose more than what you were willing to risk in the first place.

In the other hand if you read this far and not quite understood all the maths behind it and is thinking, "Oh my God I will never get it right!", you are not alone I can tell you, next chapter is for you. I will introduce you to few scripts I wrote that run in the most popular Forex trading platform, Metatrader 4. It will automatically do all the calculation for you and enter the trade with the correct Position Size. To be honest it is a tool that I use myself, knowing all that is behind the maths involved in calculating the right position size is extremely helpful, but doing it by hand when I am able to do it on the fly with any deposit account and while trading any currency pair would be just silly. It took my Position Size analysis to a whole new level.

Essential Tool For Trading

In this chapter I will briefly introduce you to a tool I developed for myself and have been using for the last 12 months to optimise my trading results. It quickly, accurately and best of all, automatically, calculates position size at the moment of entering Market and Pending orders - at the click of a button.

In the past I calculated position size manually and was sometimes a little less detail-conscious than I could have been (easy to do when you're firing off multiple trades and always more painfully obvious on losing trades!). As you now know, the calculations aren't all that complicated. But when you trade for a living it's essential to be able to manage your account and cash flow accurately, just as you would any business you owned. And as there are so many variables you can't control in business it's important to be accurate where you can.

The tool I wanted must be precise and bullet-fast. It had to work directly on my trading platform, know my Trading Account Balance and automatically calculate my position size according to my Stop Loss and percentage at risk. This tool would also need to consider the bank balance

I hold separate from my trading account (as I described in the Trading Account vs. Banking Account chapter) in these calculations.

Basically I wanted all the money management capabilities I detailed in this book to appear automatically on my trading platform!

Well they do these days. I coded the key elements of "How To Not Blow Up Your Trading Account" into a tool called Forex Profit Guard (FPG). Coded for Metatrader4, FPG takes the guesswork out of the repetitive and time consuming maths of trade management.

Although I can do all of this manually, I now have no reason to do so. My trading friends also love it. So much so that they suggested me to give it a name and make it available for everyone.

It's available at www.ForexProfitGuard.com. For those of you who bought this book there is a discount offered at this link: http://book.forexprofitguard.com/

Final Thoughts

Congratulations if you made it this far, commitment is essential. Trading is not for everyone, there is a lot to risk and no guarantees, but there is also a lot of money waiting to be made.

Don't fall for the get rich quick schemes, this is not what trading is about. The chances of you striking gold in one trade are the same of having a winning lottery ticket delivered to you by a 6 foot tall top model. Yes, it can happen but you may die waiting or quickly lose your whole account trying.

Mind you that reading this book a thousand times does not alone guarantee your success, unless you religiously follow what is in it, it is your actions that count and how you stay disciplined during good and bad times.

By applying these teachings it will for sure make you live a lot longer in the markets. If we are to die, let's postpone it as much as we can. Do not be that silly to believe in all the market fairy tales that flood your email inbox everyday, I have been there myself, believe me.

Take your time to learn the trade, it will not happen over night. Risk small, remember that you need your money to trade, if you lose it all the game is over.

What Is A Pip

If you are here straight from the POSITION SIZE chapter, good on you! It is very important that you have everything clear in your mind before you proceed into the other chapters.

Currency in the Forex business is always quoted in pairs, meaning that you measure one currency against the other.

In a currency pair you have the base and the quote. In EURUSD for instance, EUR is the base and USD the quote. It the EURUSD pair is valued at 1.3015, this means that 1.3015 USD (quote) is the equivalent of 1 Euro.

Also note that when you buy (go long) the EURUSD pair you are betting the Euro will strengthen compared to the US Dollar. In the same way you are betting that the US Dollar will devaluate compared to the Euro.

It is the exactly opposite when you sell (go short) EURUSD.

When you buy EURUSD you are long EUR and short US Dollar, or you simply are long EURUSD.

When you sell EURUSD you are short EUR and long US Dollar, or you simply are short EURUSD.

A Pip, in theory, is the smallest move a currency pair can have. You probably have noticed from your charts that currency pairs are quoted with 4 decimal places and 2 decimal places for the Japanese Yen pairs. I said in theory, because over the years Brokers found a way to divide the pip by ten, then creating the 5th digit, also known as a pipette. Do not worry too much about the pipette, we will not mention it any longer.

Let's dive straight into examples so you can quickly grasp the concept and start to do your own calculations.

Currently the EURUSD is trading around 1.3000, if the price goes up to 1.3015 you had a 15 pips increase in price. In the same way that if the new quote gives you 1.2985 you had a 15 pips decrease in value. Remember, for all the pairs not including JPY (Japanese Yen pairs), the pip is the 4th decimal place:

1.3015 − 1.3000 = 0.0015 (15 pips)
1.2985 - 1.3000 = -0.0015 (-15 pips)

An example now with a quote having the 5th digit, probably what your Broker will offer you:

1.30000 – 1.30150 = 0.00150 (15 pips). Remember that the 5th digit should not be counted. It is a decimal fraction of a pip. Pay attention to the next example:

1.30053 – 1.30008 = 0.00045 (4.5 pips)

I am sure you understood the idea, the same principle applies to the JPY pairs, but the pip in the Yen crosses are the 2nd decimal, with the 3rd being the fraction of a pip.

The NZDJPY cross is now hovering 64.000, here are few examples covering the Yen pairs.

64.20 – 64.00 = 0.20 (20 pips), 2 decimal places.
63.65 – 64.00 = -0.35 (-35 pips)

Now with the 3rd decimal, again, probably what your Broker will offer you:

64.206 – 64.015 = 0.191 (19.1 pips)

If that sounds a bit confusing to you, I urge you to take your time and understand these terminologies and simple maths. Although they may seem a bit daunting at the first read, it is actually very simple once you are acquainted to it.

Pull your notebook and jot down few examples that will help you master the basics before you can continue.

Keep In Touch

I would love to know how you are doing in trading and whether or not you were able to apply some of what I have taught you in this book.

We hear all the time that trading is a lonely business, but it does not have to be. After all this is Internet time we can all communicate in seconds, aren't we all in front of our computers? So let's keep in touch. I will get back to you as soon as I can.

You can follow me on:

Twitter: @FxPipTrader
Facebook: http://facebook.com/ForexProfitGuard
Website: http://ForexProfitGuard.com

Important Links

- Forex Profit Guard: http://forexprofitguard.com – Money Management tool for Metatrader4

- Forex Nation: http://forexnation.org - The World's 1st Not-For-Profit Broker

- Pip Gun: http://pipgun.com – My Forex Blog

Notes

Notes

Every failure brings
with it the seed of an
equivalent success.
– Napoleon Hill

Notes

Notes

We learn wisdom
from failure much
more than success.
We often discover
what we will do, by
finding out what we
will not do.
– **Samuel Smiles**

Notes

Notes

I failed my way
to success.
– **Thomas Edison**

Notes

Notes

We are what we
repeatedly do.
Excellence,
therefore, is not an
act but a habit.
– **Aristotle**

Notes

Notes

Fortune favors
the brave.
– **Publius Terence**